100 AMAZING FACTS ABOUT ALASKA

Content

Introduction 8

Fact 1 - Bigger than France and Spain combined! 9

Fact 2 - Where the sun never sets in summer 10

Fact 3 - The Mystery of the Northern Lights................................11

Fact 4 – Mount Denali, the highest peak in America 12

Fact 5 - Kodiak bears, giants of nature...13

Fact 6 - The traditional Yupik drum dance 14

Fact 7 - Alaska bought from Russia for a pittance........................15

Fact 8 - A salmon that travels a thousand miles to spawn..........16

Fact 9 - The Seal That « Sings » Under the Ice 17

Fact 10 - The Northeast Rainforest, a Green Treasure 18

Fact 11 - Whales playing hide and seek 19

Fact 12 - The Yukon River, a Route for Gold Diggers 20

Fact 13 - More than 20 words to describe snow 21

Fact 14 - The Village Moving with the Melting Ice........................22

Fact 15 - Days when the sun doesn't rise in winter......................23

Fact 16 - The Trans-Alaska Pipeline, a Black Gold Snake............24

Fact 17 - The Balto Sled Dog, a Four-Legged Hero......................25

Fact 18 - Flying reindeer... On the road..26

Fact 19 - The Winter Solstice Festival...27

Fact 20 - The Arctic Fox, a Snow Chameleon 28

Fact 21 - The Legend of the Raven, the Mischievous Bird...........29

Fact 22 - Totem Poles, the Silent Guardians of the Forests.........30

Fact 23 - Glaciers bigger than entire cities 31

Fact 24 - Caribou, the living compass of the north 32

Fact 25 - A bay where water dances in circles 33

Fact 26 - The Birth of a New Glacier 34

Fact 27 - The Ancient Art of Tattooing among the Aleuts.............35

Fact 28 - Unique Fruits and Berries...36

Fact 29 - The Music of Bowhead Whales 37

Fact 30 - The First People of Alaska Arrived 15000 Years Ago....38

Fact 31 - The Island Where Rain Reigns.......................................39

Fact 32 - The Earthquake That Moved Mountains 40

Fact 33 - Magpies, the chattering birds of the north 41

Fact 34 - The Yupiks' games of skill and balance 42

Fact 35 - The Stone Forest, a Remnant of a Bygone Era.............43

Fact 36 - Freshwater pearls as big as cherries............................44

Fact 37 - The Dance of Lights Underwater 45

Fact 38 - The Riddle of Floating Ice Circles 46

Fact 39 - Salmon that change colour...47

Fact 40 - Gold, the Brilliant Dream of the Pioneers.....................48

Fact 41 - Eagles, the Kings of the Skies of Alaska.......................49

Fact 42 - White Wolves, Ghosts of the Tundra.............................50

Fact 43 - Trees so tall you can walk in them.................................51

Fact 44 - The Well-Kept Secrets of the Ice Caves 52

Fact 45 - The Incredible Journey of the Monarch Butterflies.......53

Fact 46 - The Mystery of the Vanishing Lakes 54

3

Fact 47 - Plants that survive at -40° C..55

Fact 48 - Fish that walk on land...56

Fact 49 - Bald Eagles, Guardians of the Skies.............................57

Fact 50 - The Riddle of the Northern Penguins............................58

Fact 51 - The World Hidden Under the Icebergs...........................59

Fact 52 - The Dance of the Flying Fish...60

Fact 53 - Fish Rains, A Strange Phenomenon 61

Fact 54 - The Song of the Wolves Under the Moon......................62

Fact 55 - Whales Leapfrogging...63

Fact 56 - The Incredible Strength of the Alaskan Bison 64

Fact 57 - Applauding Seals 65

Fact 58 - Birds Dancing on Water..66

Fact 59 - The Day the River Flowed Upside Down 67

Fact 60 - The Underground Ice Maze..68

Fact 61 - The Bear Fishing by Hand...69

Fact 62 - Flowers that listen to the sun...70

Fact 63 - Foxes Playing Hide and Seek..71

Fact 64 - The Underwater Shipwreck Museum.............................72

Fact 65 - Beavers, the Architects of Rivers 73

Fact 66 - The Grizzly Bear Symphony..74

Fact 67 - Starfish illuminating the seabed....................................75

Fact 68 - The Forest That Sings with the Wind.............................76

Fact 69 - Dolphins Riding the Waves...77

Fact 70 - The Frog Orchestra in Summer 78

Fact 71 - The Labyrinth of Braided Rivers.................................79

Fact 72 - The Story of the Igloo, the Ice House 80

Fact 73 - The Legend of the Lake Iliamna Monster.................81

Fact 74 - Ephemeral Ice Sculptures..82

Fact 75 - Starry Nights That Tell Stories................................83

Fact 76 - Giant Crabs of the Deep 84

Fact 77 - The Dance of the Fireflies in Summer......................85

Fact 78 - Birds that sing non-stop 86

Fact 79 - Deer Wearing Wreaths 87

Fact 80 - The Art of Fishing with Eagles.................................88

Fact 81 - The Secret Stories of Gemstones 89

Fact 82 - The Incredible Journey of Migrating Caribou 90

Fact 83 - Seal Dance on the Ice 91

Fact 84 - The Island Where Flowers Talk 92

Fact 85 - Reindeer dancing in the snow.................................93

Fact 86 - The Story of Fire Under the Ice 94

Fact 87 - Whales Singing Songs...95

Fact 88 - Bears Dancing Under the Moon 96

Fact 89 - The Incredible Journey of Migratory Birds...............97

Fact 90 - The Stars That Tell the Future.................................98

Fact 91 - The Story of Alaska's Early Pioneers.......................99

Fact 92 - The Mystery of Moving Stones............................. 100

Fact 93 - The Island Where Time Stood Still 101

Fact 94 - The Story of the City Lost Under the Ice 102

Fact 95 - Eagles Fishing with Their Claws 103

Fact 96 - Dolphins Drawing in the Water....................................... 104

Fact 97 - Flowers that open at midnight....................................... 105

Fact 98 - The Dance of the Sea Lions Under the Waves........... 106

Fact 99 - The Story of Talking Forests 107

Fact 100 - The Mystery of the Lakes That Glow in the Night... 108

Conclusion.. 109

Quiz... 110

Answers 116

"Alaska is a great adventure, a land of wonders, but also a test, a test of strength for the heart and soul of man."

— John Muir

Introduction

Hello, dear adventurer of knowledge! Are you ready to embark on an unforgettable journey through one of the most mysterious, vast and majestic territories on our planet? Alaska, a huge state in the American Northwest, is a treasure trove of stunning natural phenomena, captivating historical facts, and deep-rooted cultural traditions.

By opening this book, you will be immersed in a universe where nature and man coexist, sometimes in harmony, sometimes in confrontation, but always in a spectacular way. Each page will reveal an amazing side of Alaska to you, whether it's through its stunning landscapes, amazing creatures, or secret stories.

Whether you're a nature enthusiast, a history buff or just a curious person looking for wonders, this book has been designed for you. As you walk through it, you'll discover 100 incredible facts that will make you see Alaska in a new light.

Be prepared, because Alaska is much more than vast expanses of snow and ice. A rich, complex and fascinating world awaits you. Let's embark on this exceptional adventure together!

Marc Dresgui

Fact 1 - Bigger than France and Spain combined!

Have you ever heard of Alaska, that faraway corner of the United States? You might think it's just a small patch of icy land up there in the North, but you'd be surprised to learn how huge it is! In fact, Alaska is the largest state in the United States, and its size is truly stunning.

Imagine that you place France above Spain, like a puzzle. Even combined, these two nations could not equal the size of Alaska! To give you an idea, Alaska covers an area of about 1.7 million square kilometers, while France and Spain, combined, occupy about 1 million square kilometers.

If you had to drive across Alaska from north to south, it would take you several days, even without making extended stops. And that's not all, as the territory is dotted with mountains, dense forests and majestic rivers.

The next time you look at a map, take a moment to measure the vastness of Alaska. It is truly a giant among states, a place where nature reigns supreme.

Fact 2 - Where the sun never sets in summer

Have you ever dreamed of a place where the day lasts forever, with no night to interrupt the light? Well, in Alaska, that dream comes true for part of the summer. It's a fascinating phenomenon called the "midnight sun," and it transforms the days into a continuous experience of light.

In the northernmost parts of Alaska, such as Barrow (or Utqiaġvik), the sun doesn't set at all for about 82 days, from late May to mid-July. Imagine: you could play outside, read a book, or do whatever you want at 2 a.m., and it would still be daylight! It may sound strange, but for Alaskans, it's a normal part of life.

However, this phenomenon also has its opposite in winter. For several weeks, the sun doesn't rise at all! It's like a long winter twilight. But in the summer, the constant glare of the sun gives Alaska a magical atmosphere.

So, if you ever go to Alaska during this time, don't forget to take thick curtains! Even though it's amazing to see the midnight sun, sometimes it's good to rest in the dark.

Fact 3 - The Mystery of the Northern Lights

Have you ever seen images of colorful lights dancing in the night sky, like mysterious luminous ribbons? It's the Northern Lights, and Alaska is one of the best places in the world to see them. These lights look like they're straight out of a fairy tale, but they actually have a scientific explanation.

The Northern Lights, also known as the Northern Lights, are caused by charged particles from the sun colliding with Earth's atmosphere. When these particles collide with the molecules in our atmosphere, they create these beautiful lights. Depending on the types of gases they encounter, different colors appear, ranging from green to pink to purple.

In places like Fairbanks in Alaska, it's common to admire these lights on clear winter nights. Many people travel from all corners of the world just for the chance to see them live.

So, if you have the opportunity to visit Alaska in the winter, don't forget to look up at the sky. You could witness one of nature's most enchanting spectacles!

Fact 4 – Mount Denali, America's Highest Peak

Did you know that Alaska is home to the highest mountain on the entire North American continent? Its name is Mount Denali, a majestic giant that reaches a dizzying height of 6,190 meters! Just thinking about it gives you chills, doesn't it? It is higher than Mount Everest when considering its base at sea level.

Now, imagine yourself climbing that mountain, crossing fields of eternal snow, and taking in breathtaking scenery. Of course, climbing to the top of Denali is an adventure reserved for experienced mountaineers due to its extreme conditions and high altitude. But this challenge pushes many climbers every year to try their luck to reach the summit.

If you visit Denali National Park, even without climbing the mountain, you'll be surrounded by spectacular wild scenery. Vast wilderness, animals such as caribou and grizzly bears, and starry night skies as far as the eye can see await you in this magical place.

What an adventure, isn't it? Alaska, with Denali, offers an escape to the rugged beauty, where nature reigns supreme and adventures abound, promising you unforgettable and uplifting experiences.

Fact 5 - Kodiak bears, giants of nature

You may have heard of brown bears, but did you know that Alaska is home to Kodiak bears, which are some of the largest bears on the planet? These impressive creatures live mainly on the Kodiak Archipelago, and they're the talk of the town!

These bears can weigh up to 680 kg or more, which is almost equivalent to the weight of 10 adults! Imagine being next to an animal of such size. Their diet consists mainly of salmon, plants, and sometimes small animals. During salmon season, they can eat huge amounts to prepare for winter.

The Kodiak Archipelago provides a perfect habitat for these bears, with vast wilderness areas, numerous fish-rich waterways, and an absence of natural predators. They are the undisputed kings of their territory.

If you ever travel to Alaska, especially the Kodiak area, you may be lucky enough to catch a glimpse of one of these giants of nature. But don't forget, always respect their space and observe them from a distance. After all, they are wild animals!

Fact 6 - The traditional Yupik drum dance

Have you ever witnessed a dance that immerses you deeply in an ancient culture and makes you feel the history? The Yupik drum dance is one of those dances that captures the essence of the Yupik culture, a Native Alaskan people. This dance is not just a movement; It's a story, a tradition, a celebration.

Accompanied by the rhythmic sound of the drum, this dance is usually performed at special events and ceremonies. Dancers wear traditional masks and handmade clothing, telling stories of hunting, fishing, healing, and everyday life. Every movement has a meaning, every step is an expression of gratitude or respect towards nature and ancestors.

The drums themselves are made from natural materials such as animal skin and wood, creating a melody that resonates deeply and has the power to connect dancers and spectators.

If you are lucky enough to see this dance live, feel the music, observe the movements and let yourself be carried away by this ancient tradition that continues to this day. This is Alaska in all its cultural beauty.

Fact 7 - Alaska bought from Russia for a pittance

Imagine, you buy a treasure for the price of a cheap toy. Unbelievable, isn't it? Well, that's exactly what happened with Alaska! In 1867, the United States made one of the biggest deals in history when it bought this huge territory from Russia.

Why did Russia want to sell Alaska? At the time, she was in financial difficulty and feared losing the area in a conflict without compensation. The agreed price? $7.2 million, or about two cents per acre. To give you an idea, it's like buying a huge castle for the price of a tiny house!

Many people criticized the purchase at the time, calling it "Seward's madness," named after the U.S. secretary of state who negotiated the deal. But over time, Alaska has proven to be a gold mine, literally and figuratively, with its wealth of natural resources.

So, the next time you think of Alaska, remember that this huge territory was acquired for a pittance. A real golden deal!

Fact 8 - A salmon that travels a thousand miles to spawn

Imagine travelling a distance equivalent to the one between Paris and Berlin, but without any means of transport, simply by the strength of your legs. That's what some salmon do in Alaska! These incredible fish sometimes travel more than a thousand miles from the ocean to their native rivers to lay their eggs.

Salmon have a remarkable sense of direction. Guided by the smell and other natural cues, he finds his way back to the river where he was born. This migration is all the more incredible when you consider how perilous this journey is, with predators at every turn and powerful currents against the current.

Once they arrive at their destination, these salmon lay their eggs and most of them die shortly thereafter. It's a sacrifice for the next generation. The new smolts will then grow in the river before launching themselves into the vast ocean.

The next time you hear about Alaskan salmon, think about this incredible journey they're doing. It's not just a fish, it's a true nature adventurer!

Fact 9 - The Seal "Singing" Under the Ice

You've heard a bird sing or a cat meow before, haven't you? But have you ever heard a seal "sing"? In Alaska, there is a type of seal, called the bearded seal, that makes strange, melodious sounds under the ice, much like a mysterious song from the depths.

These "songs" are not just for fun. They have a very specific reason! Males use these sounds during the breeding season to attract females or to establish territory. Each seal has its own unique "look", which allows females to recognize and choose their mate.

If you were to dive under the ice of Alaska during this time, you would witness a real underwater concert. With the enveloping silence of the icy waters, these songs resonate and create an almost magical atmosphere.

So, the next time you think of Alaskan animals, remember the bearded seal, that incredible singer of the deep. A wonder of nature that shows how full our world is of surprises!

Fact 10 - The Northeast Rainforest, a Green Treasure

When you think of Alaska, you probably picture snow-capped mountains, glaciers, and polar bears. But did you know that Alaska is also home to a rainforest? Yes, you read that right! Southeast Alaska has a temperate rainforest, called the Tongass National Forest.

This forest covers almost 69,000 km². It's like putting more than 13 million football fields next to each other! With its huge trees, lush mosses and crystal clear rivers, the Tongass forest is a haven of biodiversity. There are bears, eagles and even wolves!

What's fascinating is that this forest receives a huge amount of rain every year, hence the name "rainforest". Some areas can receive up to 4 metres of annual precipitation! Imagine yourself with a column of water of this height next to you.

The Tongass Forest is a reminder that Alaska isn't just ice and snow. It is a green treasure, a true paradise for nature and adventure lovers!

Fact 11 - Whales playing hide and seek

Have you ever played hide and seek? It's fun, isn't it? But did you know that some of the largest animals on our planet also play this game? In the cold waters of Alaska, humpback whales love to perform acrobatics, disappearing underwater and then suddenly popping up, as if to say "Hi, here I am!"

These majestic creatures, which can be up to 16 meters long, like to "breacher", i.e. jump out of the water before falling back down with a big splash. Why are they doing this? Scientists believe it's a means of communication, to get rid of pests or maybe just to have fun!

If you're lucky and you're near the coast of Alaska, you might even see them doing "pectoral slaps". This is when the whale slams its fin against the surface of the water, creating a resounding sound.

So, next time you're playing hide and seek, think about Alaskan whales and their water games. Even the largest animals on Earth know how to have fun and enjoy life!

Fact 12 - The Yukon River, a Route for Gold Diggers

Have you ever dreamed of finding treasure? In the 19th century, thousands of people had the same dream, and they came to Alaska, attracted by the famous Klondike Gold Rush. The Yukon River was their main route, a liquid route that led them to the gold they so desired.

This 3,190 km long river flows through Alaska and empties into the Bering Sea. During the Gold Rush, researchers used rafts, steamboats, and even canoes to navigate this huge waterway, hoping to find their fortune along its banks.

But the journey was not easy. The waters of the Yukon were fast and unpredictable, and the climate could be very harsh. Also, finding gold was anything but guaranteed. Many returned home empty-handed, while others made their fortunes.

The Yukon River is a reminder of the adventurous spirit and determination of gold prospectors. It is the silent witness to the dreams and hopes of all those who have dared to sail it, seeking to transform their lives forever.

Fact 13 - More than 20 words to describe snow

Imagine if in your language there were more than twenty words just to describe "snow". Unbelievable, right? Yet this is the case among the Inuit, the indigenous peoples of the Arctic, including Alaska. For them, snow is much more than just a blanket of white covering the ground.

Each type of snow has its own purpose and meaning. For example, there's a specific word for snow that's perfect for building an igloo, and another for one that's great for walking on. These nuances are crucial for survival in an environment as demanding as the Arctic.

This shows how deeply languages are intertwined with a people's culture and environment. The Inuit adapted their language to the nuances of their frigid daily lives, making snow a central element of their communication.

So, the next time you see snow, remember that it's not just white flakes. For some, it's a whole world of meanings, traditions, and survival.

Fact 14 - The Village Moving with the Melting Ice

Can you imagine living in a village that needs to be moved because the ground beneath your feet is melting? That's exactly what's happening in Newtok, Alaska. Because of global warming, the ice that stabilizes the ground, called permafrost, is gradually melting, making the earth unstable.

Newtok is not the only village in this situation. Several communities in Alaska are facing similar challenges, as climate change is particularly affecting this region. Melting permafrost is causing coastal erosion and threatening homes, schools and other infrastructure.

To protect its inhabitants, the solution was radical: move the entire village! Plans have been made to relocate Newtok a few miles away, on more stable ground. It's a mammoth effort that requires coordination, time, and resources.

So when you hear about climate change, remember that for some, it's not just about warmer temperatures or melting ice, it's about the very survival of their community.

Fact 15 - Days when the sun doesn't rise in winter

Have you ever imagined a day without sunshine? In Alaska, during the winter, some areas experience what is called the "polar night". This is a time when the sun doesn't show for several days or even weeks!

Barrow, Alaska's northernmost city, is a striking example. There, the sun sets at the end of November and doesn't rise until the end of January. Imagine: more than two months without seeing the light of day! This is the complete opposite of summer, where the sun never sets.

Of course, this phenomenon is due to the tilt of the Earth on its axis. The closer you get to the poles, the longer these periods of darkness or continuous light become. And despite the cold and darkness, the people of these regions have developed incredible ways to adapt and enjoy this unique time.

So, the next time you're complaining about a rainy or cloudy day, think about those endless days without sun in Alaska. It's an experience to be had, isn't it?

Fact 16 - The Trans-Alaska Pipeline, a Black Gold Snake

Did you know that Alaska has a huge "snake" that stretches for nearly 1,300 kilometers across its land? It's not a real snake, of course, but the Trans-Alaska Pipeline, a huge pipeline designed to transport oil!

Built in the 1970s, the pipeline connects the rich oil fields of Prudhoe Bay in the north to the port of Valdez in the south. It's a feat of engineering, as he has to traverse challenging terrain, mountains, rivers, and withstand the extreme Alaskan cold.

Thanks to special supports, a large part of the pipeline is raised above the ground. This allows wildlife, such as caribou, to migrate freely underneath. In addition, these supports help protect the permafrost, Alaska's frozen ground, from the heat of the oil flowing through the pipe.

So, every time you hear about Alaska's black gold, think of this gigantic "snake" silently roaming the landscape, transporting millions of barrels of oil to the rest of the world. Impressive, isn't it?

Fact 17 - The Balto Sled Dog, a Four-Legged Hero

Have you ever heard of Balto? He's not just any dog, but a true Alaskan hero. In 1925, a diphtheria epidemic threatened the lives of many residents of Nome, a remote town in Alaska. The antitoxin needed to treat the disease was hundreds of miles away, and the plane that was supposed to deliver it was grounded because of a storm.

In response to this emergency, a relay race involving sled dog teams was organized to transport the antitoxin 1085 kilometers in just five and a half days. Balto, a Siberian husky, was the lead dog of the final sled team, guiding his team on the most dangerous and difficult portion of the course.

This brave dog became a celebrity after this feat, and his determination was immortalized by a statue in New York City, in Central Park. So, the next time you hear about sled dogs in Alaska, remember Balto, the four-legged hero who saved many lives.

Fact 18 - Flying reindeer... On the road

You've probably heard of flying reindeer at Christmas, haven't you? But in Alaska, it's a different story! Here, the reindeer have an astonishing peculiarity: they cross the roads without warning, giving the impression that they are "flying" from one side to the other.

Alaska is home to a large population of wild reindeer, but these animals are also raised by local communities for meat, fur and sometimes for transportation. They regularly meet near roads or trails. If you're driving in certain areas of Alaska, you might be surprised by these fast-moving animals popping up in front of your vehicle.

As a result, local authorities and indigenous communities warn drivers and advise them to slow down, especially during hours when visibility is reduced. So, if you find yourself in Alaska, keep your eyes peeled! You may not see reindeer flying in the sky, but you might see them "flying" on the road!

Fact 19 - The Winter Solstice Festival

Have you ever experienced a moment when the night seems endless? In Alaska, during the winter solstice, that's exactly what happens. The shortest day of the year gives rise to a unique celebration, where the boundary between day and night is almost indistinguishable.

In the dead of winter, in some parts of Alaska, the sun only slightly grazes the horizon, creating a diffuse light, before disappearing again. It is a stunning natural spectacle, where darkness and light play together, providing beautiful hues in the sky.

To mark this special occasion, Alaskans created the Winter Solstice Festival. With bonfires, music, and dancing, they celebrate the light to come, anticipating the days that will gradually lengthen. It's a way to embrace the natural beauty of Alaska while defying the biting cold of winter.

If one day you find yourself in Alaska during this time, don't hesitate to join the festivities. You will have an unforgettable experience where nature and culture intertwine in a magical winter dance.

Fact 20 - The Arctic Fox, a Snow Chameleon

Imagine an animal that can change its coat to blend in perfectly with its surroundings. That's exactly what the Arctic fox does in Alaska, a true snow chameleon. Thanks to its adaptability, it survives in one of the harshest climates on the planet.

In winter, the Arctic fox sports a pristine white coat, allowing it to camouflage itself in snow and ice. This discretion is essential for hunting and protecting oneself from predators. But when the seasons change and the tundra begins to turn green, the fur of this small mammal turns into a brown or gray coat, blending with rocks and vegetation.

This color change isn't just aesthetic. It is vital for the fox. By blending in with its environment, it can approach its prey undetected and evade those who hunt it. It's an amazing adaptation that nature has given him.

The next time you hear about the Arctic fox, remember this incredible ability to become one with its environment. It's a testament to the magic and wonder of the Alaskan wilderness.

Fact 21 - The Legend of the Raven, the Mischievous Bird

At the heart of Alaskan myths and legends is the raven, a black-plumaged bird known for its cunning and mischief. In Indigenous cultures, he is often seen as a hero, a creator, but also a scoundrel. Its dual nature gives it a special place in stories passed down from generation to generation.

One of the most famous legends portrays him as the liberator of the light of the world. According to tradition, a powerful leader kept all the lights locked in a box. The raven, through his cunning, managed to get hold of this box and released the light, thus illuminating the world. This is how he is also seen as a benefactor.

But the raven is also known for its pranks. There are many stories where he deceives other animals to satisfy his own needs or simply to have fun. His shrewd personality makes him both admired and feared.

So, if you're visiting Alaska and spot a raven, remember its important place in local folklore. More than just a bird, it is a living symbol of the mysteries and magic of this faraway land.

Fact 22 - Totem Poles, the Silent Guardians of the Forests

As you walk through the dense forests of Alaska, you might come across strange and fascinating sculptures: totem poles. These slender poles, adorned with carved figures, are more than just works of art. They are custodians of the histories, traditions, and beliefs of the Indigenous peoples of the region.

Each totem pole tells a story. Whether it's a family's lineage, a historical event, or a myth, each figure, animal or human, engraved on the pole has a specific meaning. For example, the eagle, often depicted at the top of the totem pole, symbolizes peace and protection.

These works are not just spiritual representations. They also serve as territorial markers or memorials. Some totem poles may even depict events or treaties between different tribes, immortalizing crucial moments in local history.

The next time you come face to face with one of these silent guardians, take a moment to admire it. Behind every sculpted detail is a story, a lesson, a fragment of the Alaskan soul.

Fact 23 - Glaciers bigger than entire cities

Have you ever imagined a block of ice stretching for miles, rivaling metropolises in size? In Alaska, this isn't just an image, it's a reality. The glaciers here are not just ice caps, but true giants stretching over territories as vast as cities.

The Malaspina Glacier, for example, covers an area of about 3,900 km², which is larger than the state of Rhode Island! Standing in front of it, you'll feel tiny, dominated by this sea of ice that seems to stretch to infinity.

These glaciers are not only impressive in their size. They play a crucial role in the ecosystem. As they melt, they feed rivers and lakes, creating habitats for many species. It is in these glacier-fed waters that salmon begin their incredible migratory journey.

The next time you hear about Alaska's glaciers, imagine icy expanses larger than entire cities, shaping the landscape and sustaining life in unimaginable ways.

Fact 24 - Caribou, the living compass of the north

You may have heard of Santa's reindeer before, but did you know that these creatures actually exist in Alaska under the name of caribou? These majestic animals, with their large horns and graceful appearance, are much more than just a Christmas icon.

Caribou are not only beautiful to look at, they have an incredible ability to orient themselves. Each year, they undertake one of the longest overland migrations, traveling thousands of miles through tundra, mountains, and forests. Imagine, some groups of caribou travel distances equivalent to a round trip between Paris and Moscow!

This migration is a vital necessity. It allows caribou to find food during harsh winters and escape predators. These trips also have a profound impact on the ecosystem, as they contribute to seed dispersal and vegetation renewal.

So, the next time you think of reindeer during the holidays, remember the caribou, the living compass that braves the elements every year to make its way through the vastness of Alaska.

Fact 25 - A bay where water dances in circles

Have you ever seen water swirling in a bathtub? Now imagine a huge expanse of water dancing in gigantic circles. Welcome to Alaska's Cook's Bay, home to some of the world's most impressive tidal currents.

Cook's Bay is like a huge natural amphitheatre where the tides play the main role. Twice a day, huge amounts of water flow in and out of this narrow bay, creating powerful currents that can reach speeds of 8 to 10 knots. To give you an idea, it's faster than most people can swim!

These tidal currents are not only an impressive sight to observe, they also play a crucial role in the local ecosystem. They provide essential nutrients that feed plankton, which in turn, feeds fish and other sea creatures.

The next time you're standing by a quiet beach, think of this distant bay where the water dances in a tumultuous ballet, reminding us of the indomitable force of nature.

Fact 26 - The Birth of a New Glacier

Have you ever thought about how a glacier comes to be? In Alaska, the magic of nature brings these ice giants to life, and the process is absolutely fascinating. Glaciers are born from snow that accumulates over years and, under its own weight, compacts to form ice.

In the mountainous regions of Alaska, when snow falls faster than it melts or undergoes sublimation, a thick layer accumulates. Over time, this layer of snow becomes denser and denser, pushing the air bubbles out and turning the snow into a crystalline blue mass: the glacier.

A fascinating example is the Hubbard Glacier. This giant continues to grow, stretching over 120 kilometers long. Its front, where it meets the sea, often has impressive breaks, where huge blocks of ice fall into the ocean.

So, the next time you see an image of a glistening glacier, remember the long and incredible journey it took from its first snowflake to its majestic stature.

Fact 27 - The Ancient Art of Tattooing among the Aleuts

Have you ever heard of traditional Aleut tattoos? Long before tattooing became a global trend, the Alaskan Aleuts had already embraced this body art as an integral part of their culture. For them, it was not just a decoration, but a rite of passage and a sign of belonging.

The tattooed designs varied greatly from person to person, and their meaning was profound. Some designs depicted family totems, personal achievements, or connections to natural elements, such as animals or weather phenomena. An individual with a wolf tattoo, for example, could be recognized as a skilled hunter.

In addition to their symbolic significance, these tattoos served as protection. The Aleuts believed that tattoos could repel evil spirits and bring good luck and strength to the wearer. These marks were often made during special ceremonies, using traditional tools and natural inks.

The next time you see a tattoo, remember that beyond aesthetics, there can be a whole cultural heritage and deeply held beliefs.

Fact 28 - Unique Fruits and Berries

Have you ever tasted berries that you wouldn't find anywhere else in the world? Alaska is a land of botanical wonders. Thanks to its unique climate and rich soils, some plants have evolved there in distinct ways.

Take, for example, the cloudberry berry, also known as the sun berry. It loves the cold bogs of Alaska and, when ripe, offers a flavor that is both sweet and tangy. It's a little wonder that you will only taste in these northern lands. Another treasure is the crowberry berry, a shiny, black, pearl-like fruit that is rich in antioxidants.

But that's not all. In addition to berries, there are fruits such as kiwai, a variety of kiwi that is specific to Alaska. It's smaller than the usual kiwi, but just as delicious, with a smooth skin that can be eaten.

So, if you ever find yourself in Alaska, don't forget to look for these natural delights. It's a taste experience you won't soon forget!

Fact 29 - The Music of Bowhead Whales

Did you know that the Arctic Ocean resonates with mystical melodies? If you listen, you might hear the music of bowhead whales. These giants of the seas, also known as Greenland whales, sing intricate songs that spread across the vast expanses of water.

Each whale has its own melodic signature, and they use these songs to communicate with each other, whether it's to orient themselves, find mates, or simply express their emotions. These melodies can last for several minutes and vary in frequency, ranging from low to high-pitched sounds.

Researchers have even found that these songs evolve over time. For example, a whale might introduce a new note or change a melodic sequence from one year to the next. It's an ever-evolving art form, just like our human music.

So, next time you're visiting the cold waters of Alaska, keep your ears open. You could be the privileged spectator of an exceptional underwater concert offered by these maestros of the deep.

Fact 30 - The First People of Alaska Arrived 15000 Years Ago

Have you ever imagined what Alaska was like millennia ago? Long before modern explorers set foot on this wild land, men and women were already walking on these lands. The first inhabitants of Alaska arrived about 15,000 years ago, a time when the world was much different from the one you know.

These ancestors, who came from present-day Siberia, crossed the Bering Strait, which was then dry land due to lower water levels during the last ice age. Equipped with stone tools and ancestral know-how, they hunted woolly mammoths, fished in frozen rivers and set up the first camps under the boreal sky.

Over time, these peoples gave rise to various Alaska Native cultures and tribes, each with its own traditions, languages, and customs. The Athabascans, Yupiks, Aleuts, and many others are descended from these early inhabitants.

So whenever you take in the vastness of Alaska, remember the footsteps of the first explorers who, 15,000 years ago, first discovered this land.

Fact 31 - The Island Where Rain Reigns

Have you ever heard of a place where rain dominates almost every day of the year? Welcome to Ketchikan, located on Revillagigedo Island in Alaska. This city is often referred to as the "rain capital of the world".

Ketchikan receives an average of more than 380 centimetres of precipitation per year, making it one of the wettest areas in North America. Here, the umbrella is a must-have accessory and the inhabitants have developed an incredible resilience in the face of this capricious weather. Their daily lives are punctuated by the gentle sound of rain falling on the rooftops and the surrounding forests.

This abundance of rain, however, has its advantages. It feeds many rivers and waterfalls, making the area lush and fertile. The forests of Ketchikan are dense and verdant, providing an ideal habitat for a variety of wildlife.

So, if you decide to visit this singular place, don't forget your raincoat! And take the time to appreciate this unique atmosphere where the rain, although often present, adds to the beauty and mystique of the island.

Fact 32 - The Earthquake That Moved Mountains

Do you know the most powerful earthquake ever recorded in North America? It was in Alaska on March 27, 1964. On that day, the earth rumbled with unimaginable force, shaking the ground and shaking the mountains.

With a magnitude of 9.2 on the Richter scale, this quake, known as the Good Friday quake, lasted nearly five minutes. That's almost an eternity when it comes to earthquakes. Imagine the streets cracking and buildings collapsing around you during that time.

It wasn't just the earth that moved. The earthquake caused devastating tsunamis that reached heights of up to 67 meters in some places. These waves ravaged the coast of Alaska, washing away everything in their path, and even caused damage in places as far away as California and Japan.

So, the next time you walk on Alaskan soil, remember that dormant force that lies dormant beneath. It has the power to reshape entire landscapes in a matter of minutes.

Fact 33 - Magpies, the chattering birds of the north

If you're walking around Alaska, chances are you'll come across the chattering magpie, a quick-witted and very communicative bird. With its bright black and white plumage, it does not go unnoticed. But it's not so much her appearance that sets her apart, it's her voice.

The magpie is one of the few birds that can imitate other sounds, whether from other animals or even mechanical noises. This talent sometimes earned him the reputation of being a real little clown of the Alaskan forests. Some locals will even tell you that they have heard a magpie imitate the ringing of a telephone!

But these birds aren't just imitators. They possess remarkable intelligence. They are able to solve complex problems and have even been seen using tools to get food. It's fascinating to think that this bird, often associated with tales and legends, has such an adaptability.

So, if you hear an unexpected chatter or noise on your next trip to Alaska, look up. You might just run into one of these mischievous magpies, ready to play a little sound trick on you.

Fact 34 - The Yupiks' games of skill and balance

As you immerse yourself in Alaskan culture, you'll learn about the Yupiks, a native Alaskan people, and their fascinating traditional games that are much more than just entertainment. These games are a reflection of their daily lives, mixing skill, endurance and strategy, inherited from generation to generation.

One of these games, the "Nalukataq", requires great strength and an impeccable sense of balance. Participants stand on taut skin and are thrown into the air by the group, trying to perform tricks before falling back down. These movements mimic the hunting and jumping of wild animals. Imagine the show!

Another game, the "Yuraq", is a dance that tells stories. Every movement has a meaning, whether it's caribou hunting or bird migration. The dancers wear traditional masks and costumes, making each performance unique.

Next time you're in Alaska, take some time to check out these games and dances. They will give you a deep insight into the Yupik culture, and who knows, maybe you'll get the opportunity to participate and test your own balance!

Fact 35 - The Stone Forest, a Remnant of a Bygone Era

Imagine walking in the middle of a forest where trees are turned to stones. In Alaska, such a place exists and it is a breathtaking sight. This stone forest is actually a field of petrified tree fossils, frozen in time for millions of years.

When these trees lived, Alaska had a very different climate. Over the years, volcanic eruptions and geological changes have buried these trees under a layer of ash and sediment. Under these conditions, the organic materials of the trees were slowly replaced by minerals, turning them into stone statues.

This stone forest is more than just a field of rocks. It offers a glimpse into Alaska's prehistoric past, a testament to climatic and geological changes. Each petrified trunk tells an ancient story, a fragment of Earth's history.

Next time you're exploring Alaska, look for this mystical forest. Every step you take there will transport you back to a time when dinosaurs still roamed the Earth. A trip back in time not to be missed!

Fact 36 - Freshwater pearls as big as cherries

Have you ever held a freshwater pearl between your fingers? In Alaska, you might be surprised! Some Alaskan lakes and rivers are home to freshwater mussels that produce surprisingly large pearls, comparable to the size of juicy cherries.

These pearls, shaped by nature, form when tiny intrusive particles enter the molds and are slowly coated with layers of mother-of-pearl, the shiny material that makes up the shell's interior. Over time, the mother-of-pearl accumulates, forming these massive, dazzling pearls.

These natural gems, both rare and valuable, are highly sought after by collectors and jewelry designers around the world. Their unique color and impressive size make them distinctive and highly desirable.

Next time you're out and about Alaskan waters, keep an eye out! You might discover one of these natural wonders. An Alaskan pearl, a true treasure of nature, may be waiting to be found by a curious explorer like you.

Fact 37 - The Dance of Lights Underwater

Alaska, with its Northern Lights, already fascinates you with its play of lights in the sky, doesn't it? But did you know that the depths of its waters also offer a breathtaking light show? Immerse yourself in the mystical world of marine bioluminescence.

This enchanting phenomenon is caused by marine organisms, such as some jellyfish and small crustaceans, which emit light, usually blue-green, in response to disturbances in their environment. Imagine swimming in a sea of shooting stars, each movement causing an explosion of light.

The coastal areas and deep bays of Alaska, especially around the Inside Passage region, are particularly conducive to these appearances. Night kayakers and divers often witness these luminescent ballets.

So, next time you're in Alaska, consider exploring not only the sky, but also the depths of the sea. Let yourself be carried away by this dance of lights, another well-kept secret of this land of wonders.

Fact 38 - The Riddle of Floating Ice Circles

Have you ever heard of the mysterious ice circles floating on Alaskan waters? These rotating circular formations have long been a source of intrigue for locals and researchers. Imagine a huge disc of ice, slowly spinning on its axis, lost in the middle of a body of water.

Their creation is a fascinating natural spectacle. When temperatures drop rapidly, the cold water in a river or lake, laden with ice particles, begins to freeze in a circle. The current, interacting with the temperature, shapes this perfect circle.

One of the most famous ice circles has been observed on the Susitna River in Alaska, attracting curious onlookers from all over the world. With an impressive diameter, this disc seemed almost unearthly, spinning silently on the tranquil waters.

If you're lucky enough to visit Alaska in the winter, keep an eye out for this amazing phenomenon. This is another wonder that this icy land has in store for those who know where to look.

Fact 39 - Salmon that change colour

Have you ever noticed the fascinating change in colour of salmon when they return to Alaskan rivers to spawn? This is not a mere fantasy of nature, but an evolutionary spectacle in action. Initially, these fish usually exhibit a silvery tinge when they live in the sea.

However, as the spawning season approaches, an incredible transformation occurs. Depending on the species and maturity, salmon can take on colours ranging from pink to deep red, with mottling and spotting. This mutation is linked to the production of hormones, preparing the fish for its last vital mission: reproduction.

A striking example is the sockeye salmon, whose skin turns scarlet red and the eyes green during spawning. This transformation is not only a visual spectacle, but it also serves to attract partners and intimidate rivals.

The next time you visit Alaska, keep a close eye on these creatures. Their journey and transformation are a reflection of the pure magic of nature.

Fact 40 - Gold, the Brilliant Dream of the Pioneers

Alaska often conjures up images of vast wilderness landscapes, but did you know that it was also the scene of one of the greatest gold rushes in history? It all began in the late nineteenth century, with the discovery of gold in the Klondike, dragging thousands of adventurers into a frantic race for riches.

In Skagway and Dawson City, tents sprang up almost overnight, forming bustling towns of gold prospectors, entrepreneurs, and dreamers. Some have become wealthy, but many have lost everything, victims of the unforgiving climate or fierce competition. The story of Soapy Smith, the legendary con man from Skagway, illustrates the survival of the fittest that prevailed at the time.

But beyond these stories of quick fortunes, it is the pioneering spirit that best characterizes this period. Determined men and women, ready to do anything to seize their chance in hostile territory.

Today, you can still find traces of that golden era by visiting historic towns or immersing yourself in the tales of the daring pioneers who shaped Alaska.

Fact 41 - Eagles, the Kings of the Skies of Alaska

Have you ever looked up at the sky in Alaska and seen a tall, majestic figure hovering overhead? It was probably a golden eagle or bald eagle, birds that embody the power and freedom of Alaska's skies. These impressive birds have a wingspan of up to more than two metres, and they dominate the aerial landscape of the region.

A place particularly famous for its eagles is the town of Haines. Every year, thousands of eagles migrate to the Chilkat River, attracted by the abundant salmon. This concentration of eagles is such that it offers one of the largest gatherings of eagles in the world. Imagine the incredible spectacle of seeing these winged giants dive into the water to catch their prey!

But these eagles are not only a wonder to behold, they also play a vital role in the ecosystem. As predators at the top of the food chain, they help regulate the populations of other animals and maintain the balance of nature.

Whenever you see one of these kings of the skies, remember that they are the living emblem of wild and free Alaska.

Fact 42 - White Wolves, Ghosts of the Tundra

As you traverse the vast expanse of Alaskan tundra, there's an elusive creature that might just cross your path: the white wolf, also known as the Arctic wolf. Blessed with thick, white fur, this beautiful animal blends in perfectly with snowy landscapes, earning it the nickname "Ghost of the Tundra."

These wolves are not only notable for their distinctive coats. Their ability to adapt is equally impressive. While many animals migrate or hibernate to escape the bitter cold, these wolves remain active throughout the winter, braving temperatures that can dip well below freezing. Their secret? An extra layer of fat and dense fur that insulates them from the cold.

But their survival doesn't stop there. These wolves are fearsome hunters, working in packs to track and capture their prey, from caribou to arctic hares. Their hunting technique is a mix of patience, strategy, and stamina.

So, next time you're standing on the tundra, keep your eyes peeled. You might witness the silent ballet of the white wolf, the true specter of the Alaskan wilderness.

Fact 43 - Trees so tall you can walk in them

You might think it's the scenario of a fantasy tale, but in Alaska, some trees are so massive that they seem like portals to another world. These giants stand majestically, some of them reaching millennial ages and having survived many environmental challenges.

These colossi of nature are often hollow inside, victims of lightning or disease, creating huge cavities. It is not uncommon to see curious or adventurous people walking inside these trunks, marveling at the space offered by these trees. Some, like the western red cedar, have cavities so large that you could hold a small meeting in them!

It's not just their size that impresses, but also the rich history they hold. Each ring on their trunk tells a story of a year of their existence, and some of these giants have seen civilizations rise and fall.

So, if one day you find yourself in front of one of these majestic trees in Alaska, take a moment to admire. Not only are they a feat of nature, but they are also the silent custodians of Earth's history.

Fact 44 - The Well-Kept Secrets of the Ice Caves

Imagine yourself entering a fairytale world, where the walls glow an intense blue and the silence is broken only by the gentle dripping of water. This is the experience offered by Alaska's ice caves, natural wonders formed by the movement of glaciers.

These caves, sculpted by time, water and wind, offer a breathtaking spectacle. Daylight penetrates the ice, making it sparkle with a thousand lights. A striking example is Mendenhall Cave, near Juneau, where you can admire ice vaults stretching as far as the eye can see.

But these caves are not just jewels for the eyes. They also hold geological secrets, telling the story of the region's glacial movements. Some researchers even find unique microorganisms there, which evolved in this isolated and extreme environment.

If you have the opportunity to visit one of these natural cathedrals, be careful. Ice can be treacherous, and it's essential to be well equipped. But one thing's for sure: you'll be amazed by the raw and pure magic of Alaskan nature.

Fact 45 - The Incredible Journey of the Monarch Butterflies

Have you ever heard of the exceptional journey of monarch butterflies? These delicate creatures, known for their bright orange wings, undertake one of the longest migrations in the animal world.

Every year, these butterflies travel thousands of kilometres, from Canada and the United States to the mountainous forests of Mexico. This journey is all the more impressive when you consider that these butterflies weigh little more than a feather. During their journey, they use air currents to save energy, soaring and dancing in the sky.

Their journey is not simply a quest for warmth. It's also a matter of survival. Monarchs migrate to escape the freezing temperatures of the North American winter, which would be fatal for them. When they reach Mexico, they find refuge in the oyamel forests, forming amazing clusters of colorful wings.

Their incredible journey is an eloquent demonstration of nature's perseverance in the face of challenges. As you observe these butterflies, you'll realize that even the smallest beings are capable of unimaginable feats.

Fact 46 - The Mystery of the Vanishing Lakes

Would it be possible for you to imagine an entire lake disappearing overnight? In Alaska, this strange and captivating phenomenon is actually happening. Thermal lakes are unique aqueous formations that can disappear in the space of a few days or weeks.

These lakes are formed by the melting of permafrost ice. Water accumulates, forming beautiful lakes on the surface of the ground. However, with global warming, permafrost is melting at an unprecedented rate, causing changes in the underlying soil. If the ground subsides or a cavity forms, the water runs off, and the lake can literally drain.

For example, Goldstream Lake, located near Fairbanks, was almost completely emptied in a two-week span in 2018. Residents watched in amazement as the water flowed through a network of crevices until the lake was a memory.

These ephemeral lakes are a reminder of the fragility of our ecosystems and the undeniable impact of climate change on nature. When you visit Alaska, you may well witness these fascinating and disturbing transformations.

Fact 47 - Plants that survive at -40°C

Have you ever imagined how plants could survive in the freezing cold of -40° C? In Alaska, some plants have evolved in surprising ways to withstand these extreme temperatures. They are a living example of nature's adaptability in the face of climate challenges.

First, many of these plants have accelerated life cycles. From the first signs of spring, they germinate, flower and fruit in record time to take advantage of the short summer period. The cottongrass, for example, unfurls its fine white feathers as soon as the temperatures allow, offering a contrasting spectacle on the frozen ground.

In addition, many of these plants adopt a low, rosette or cushion posture to protect themselves from the icy wind and take advantage of the warmth of the soil. The arctic willow, for example, grows little taller than your ankle, but spreads horizontally to maximize its light capture.

The next time you set foot on Alaskan soil, remember to look beneath your feet. You will discover a mosaic of life, testifying to the incredible resilience of nature in the face of the adversity of the cold.

Fact 48 - Fish that walk on land

You'd be surprised to know that in Alaska, some fish can literally "walk" on land! These incredible creatures once again demonstrate the ability of the natural world to adapt to particularly demanding environments.

The Alaskan wolffish, for example, uses its sturdy pectoral fins to move through shallow water and even mud. It does this to gain access to areas rich in food or to escape predators. Imagine a fish, moving in the water, making its way through the swampy terrain to continue its search for food!

These fish have modified lungs that allow them to extract oxygen from the air. So even out of the water, they aren't left out of breath. It's a fascinating ability that shows nature's determination to survive, no matter the circumstances.

So, on your next visit to Alaska, keep your eyes peeled and your ears strained. Who knows? You could witness this amazing sight: a fish walking out of its natural element.

Fact 49 - Bald Eagles, Guardians of the Skies

Have you ever looked up at the sky in Alaska and seen a majestic figure soaring high in the air? It is probably the bald eagle, the national emblem of the United States and the true guardian of Alaska's skies.

This impressive bird of prey has a wingspan of up to 2.3 metres. With its white head and tail contrasting with the rest of its dark brown body, it's hard to miss. It is not uncommon to see them diving at full speed towards the water to catch a fish with fearsome accuracy.

Alaska is home to the largest population of bald eagles in North America. Coastal areas, lakes and rivers are their favorite playgrounds, where they can be seen perched on tall pine trees or soaring above the waters.

So, next time you're visiting Alaska, take a moment to admire these incredible birds. Their elegance in flight and their essential role in the ecosystem will remind you how unique and precious Alaska's nature is.

Fact 50 - The Riddle of the Northern Penguins

You might be surprised to learn that despite the popular images, there are no penguins in Alaska. Yes, you read that right! Penguins are native to the southern hemisphere, especially Antarctica. So where does this common confusion come from?

Alaska is actually home to the "thick-billed murre" and other seabirds that resemble penguins. These creatures, while having a similar appearance, differ greatly in their habits and habitats. Unlike penguins, these birds are excellent thieves and can often be seen hovering over icy waters.

The name "penguin" was once used to refer to some northern hemisphere birds that are now extinct. This outdated terminology likely contributed to the persistent confusion between murres and penguins.

The next time you're in Alaska and think you've spotted a "penguin," take a closer look. You're likely to discover one of these fascinating northern birds that, while different, are just as captivating to watch.

Fact 51 - The World Hidden Under the Icebergs

When you see an iceberg in Alaska, you're really just seeing the tip of the iceberg. About 90% of its mass is hidden underwater, concealing a fascinating and mysterious ecosystem. These ice monoliths are much more than just floating chunks of ice.

Beneath these icy mountains, a multitude of creatures find refuge. For example, starfish, anemones and shrimp attach themselves directly to the ice, while other species, such as halibut, hide in the shadows of the iceberg to surprise their prey. These mobile icebergs become oases of life in a sometimes desolate ocean.

In addition to providing habitat, icebergs also play a crucial role in regulating ocean temperature. They release fresh water when they melt, which can influence ocean currents and climate on a much larger scale.

The next time you see an iceberg, remember that it's not only a beautiful sight, but also a complex and vital ecosystem that influences marine life in ways you never imagined.

Fact 52 - The Dance of the Flying Fish

If you believe that fish can only live underwater, Alaskan waters will prove you wrong. The flying fish, which frequent these waters, possess an astonishing ability to glide out of the water, propelling themselves with strength and elegance above the waves.

Why do these fish do this? In reality, it's a survival strategy. When chased by predators, they use their long, wide pectoral fins to "fly" out of the water, sometimes traveling an impressive distance. In the air, they can reach surprising speeds, allowing them to evade threats such as larger fish or seabirds.

But this aerial dance is not just an escape. It's also a fascinating sight to watch, especially when a group of flying fish launch themselves out of the water together, creating a synchronized choreography against the blue sky.

Next time you're standing by Alaskan waters, keep an eye on the horizon. You could witness this incredible dance, a spectacle offered by nature itself.

Fact 53 - Fish Rains, A Strange Phenomenon

Alaska is not only famous for its majestic landscapes and varied wildlife. It's also the place where you might witness a fascinating phenomenon: a rain of fish. Yes, you heard that right. Sometimes fish literally fall from the sky.

This phenomenon, as incredible as it may seem, has a scientific explanation. During severe thunderstorms or tornadoes, winds can suck fish out of the water of lakes, rivers, or the sea. Once in the air, these fish are carried by the wind, sometimes over long distances.

When the storm passes or the tornado dissipates, these fish are then dumped on the ground like rain. Imagine for a moment walking around and seeing dozens, if not hundreds, of fish falling around you. It's an experience that few people can recount.

So, if you ever find yourself in Alaska in the pouring rain, take a good look around. You might be surprised by what heaven has in store for you!

Fact 54 - The Song of the Wolves Under the Moon

Alaska, a wild and mysterious land, is home to many wolves that roam its vast expanses. But do you know what makes these Alaskan nights even more mesmerizing? The melodious and captivating song of wolves under the silvery glow of the moon.

When night falls, you might be lucky to hear those distant calls. It's not just a howl, it's a complex communication between pack members. These songs are used to strengthen social ties, to mark their territory or to coordinate their hunts.

It is fascinating to know that each wolf has a unique voice, allowing its conspecifics to identify it. For example, when a young wolf gets lost, it may howl for adults to find it with its distinct voice.

If you're lucky enough to camp in Alaska, and the moon is lighting up the landscape, keep an ear out. Let yourself be lulled by this natural concert and feel the magic of the wild nature that surrounds you.

Fact 55 - Whales Leapfrogging

Have you ever seen a multi-ton animal doing acrobatics in the air? Alaska has this mind-boggling spectacle in store for you! There, it is not uncommon to observe whales leaping out of the water, providing a breathtaking sight.

This phenomenon is called "breaching", and while the exact reasons are not fully understood, several theories exist. Some scientists believe that whales do this to get rid of parasites or to communicate with other members of their group.

Imagine the scene: you're admiring the calm of the ocean, when suddenly, a majestic whale appears, defying gravity, before falling heavily into a splinter of water. It's an impressive display of strength and agility for an animal of this size.

Next time you're visiting Alaska, keep an eye on the horizon. If you're lucky, you'll witness this giant leapfrog game, one of the many miracles Alaskan wilderness has to offer.

Fact 56 - The Incredible Strength of the Alaskan Bison

Have you ever heard of the Alaskan bison? This massive animal is the symbol of raw power in the animal kingdom. Although more associated with the plains of North America, Alaska is home to a robust population of these giants.

Alaskan bison can weigh up to 1,000 kilograms, making them one of the largest terrestrial herbivores. To give you an idea, it's like ten average-sized adults coming together in a single muscle entity! And with this force, they can run up to 55 km/h.

But this strength isn't just for running. In the harsh Alaskan wilderness, bison use their power to make their way through deep snow, to fight predators, or even to establish dominance in fighting rituals with other males.

So, on your next visit to Alaska, if you're lucky, you might catch a glimpse of one of these behemoths in action. But a word of advice: admire them from afar, because their power is as impressive as it is formidable!

Fact 57 - Applauding Seals

Do you know the natural spectacle that some Alaskan seals offer? No, it's not a circus act, but rather a fascinating habit: these sea creatures have the art of "clapping" with their fins!

This behaviour, which resembles applause, has a very specific reason. In fact, male seals, in particular, use this method to attract the attention of females during the mating season. It's a way for them to say, "Look at me, I'm the best choice!"

But it's not just a game of seduction. These snaps also serve to scare away potential predators. By producing a loud and unexpected sound, seals can surprise and repel intruders, ensuring their safety and that of their young.

Next time you're near the Alaskan coast, keep your ears open. Maybe you'll witness this amazing aquatic performance. And don't forget, behind every snap is a story of survival, love and instinct!

Fact 58 - Birds Dancing on Water

Can you imagine a bird that can dance on the surface of the water? In Alaska, this spectacle is not just an illusion, but an incredible reality! Several species of birds, such as phalaropes, perform this intoxicating water dance.

Their technique is both graceful and functional. By spinning rapidly on themselves, these birds create a small whirlpool in the water. This movement attracts small creatures to the surface on which they feed, such as insects or tiny crustaceans. So it's a clever hunting strategy!

If you have the chance to observe this aquatic ballet, you will notice how skilled these birds are. Their fast, coordinated movements allow them to stay balanced while capturing their prey with surgical precision.

So, on your next visit to Alaska, keep your eyes on the water. Who knows, you might be the privileged spectator of one of the most beautiful natural dances in the animal kingdom!

Fact 59 - The Day the River Flowed Upside Down

Have you ever heard of a river that suddenly changes direction and flows backwards? It may seem implausible, but in Alaska, nature is capable of mind-boggling feats. One such anomaly occurred as a result of a powerful earthquake.

In 1964, Alaska was rocked by the most powerful earthquake ever recorded in North America. With a magnitude of 9.2, it caused considerable damage and reshaped part of the Alaskan landscape. In some areas, the ground has risen or subsided, changing the course of some rivers.

In some places, the water, blocked by the new elevations, began to flow in the opposite direction, giving the impression that the river had reversed. This transformation, however, was only temporary. Once the water found a new path, the current returned to normal.

This phenomenon is a powerful reminder of the power of nature in Alaska and its ability to redraw its own landscapes in an instant.

Fact 60 - The Underground Ice Maze

Have you ever wondered what lies beneath the vast, frozen expanses of Alaska? Beneath the towering ice caps, a mysterious world stretches out, made up of tunnels and caverns sculpted by time. Alaska's underground ice maze is a breathtaking natural masterpiece.

Alaskan glaciers, in constant motion, are digging and shaping the underlying soil. The meltwater, as it flows, sculpts winding tunnels that form a complex network of passages. Some of these tunnels are so large that they can accommodate one person, or even a small group of people. Inside, the play of light creates hypnotic bluish hues, reflecting the purity and density of the ice.

Daring explorers who dare to venture into these caves discover a silent and bewitching universe. But be careful! This world is constantly changing. The ice melts, moves, and reforms, altering the landscape almost daily.

If you're an adventurer at heart, this maze offers a unique experience. However, never forget to respect the power and unpredictability of this wilderness.

Fact 61 - The Bear Fishing by Hand

Have you ever seen a really skilled fisherman? In Alaska, some of the best anglers aren't human, they're bears! These giants, especially the Alaskan brown bear, have developed a surprisingly efficient and spectacular fishing technique.

Every summer, when salmon swim up rivers to spawn, bears are stationed in strategic areas where the current is strong. Armed with their sharp claws and remarkable patience, they wait for the right moment. And then, in a flash, their paw dives into the water, catching the fish with impressive accuracy.

It's not just about hunger, it's also an art. Each bear has its own technique. Some prefer to stand on rocks, while others put themselves squarely in the water, becoming an obstacle themselves that the fish have to get around.

If you're lucky enough to visit Alaska during salmon migration season, don't miss this fascinating sight. But always remember to keep a safe distance. After all, you're in the territory of the bear, the true master fisherman.

Fact 62 - Flowers that listen to the sun

Did you know that some flowers in Alaska seem to have the ability to "listen" to the sun? In this state where the days can be surprisingly long or incredibly short depending on the season, the flora has adapted surprising behaviors to maximize their exposure to light.

Heliotropes, for example, are those fascinating flowers that follow the sun across the sky. Each morning, they turn east, catching the first rays, and then slowly rotate westward as the day progresses. This daily dance allows them to absorb as much sunlight as possible, optimizing their photosynthesis process.

But that's not all. When the sun doesn't really set during the summer, as it does in some parts of Alaska, these flowers stay awake, following the sun for almost 24 hours straight. Imagine the dedication!

If you're traveling to Alaska during the summer months, take a moment to observe this natural ballet. These flowers, in perfect synchronization with the sun, will remind you of the magic and adaptability of nature.

Fact 63 - Foxes Playing Hide and Seek

Have you ever heard of foxes playing hide and seek in Alaska? These cunning little predators have developed amazing behaviors to survive in the vast wilderness of this state.

During the winter months, the Alaskan red fox uses its keen sense of hearing to locate its prey hidden under the snow. When it detects a small rodent, it jumps high into the air and dives headfirst into deep snow, often successfully! To an observer, this behavior looks suspiciously like a game of hide-and-seek where the fox is both the seeker and the winner.

But the game doesn't end there. Sometimes these cunning foxes hide their prey to consume later. They use their snouts to dig small hiding places in the snow or ground, burying their treasure in them.

So, if you're walking around Alaska and notice foxes happily bouncing or snooping through the snow, remember that they're masters of the art of hide and seek. A natural spectacle that will show you how clever and playful wildlife can be.

Fact 64 - The Underwater Shipwreck Museum

Alaska, with its winding coastlines and sometimes unpredictable waters, holds a submerged historical treasure that you might find fascinating. Let's dive into the depths to discover the Alaskan Underwater Shipwreck Museum.

For centuries, the waters surrounding Alaska have been the scene of many shipwrecks. From fishing boats caught in sudden storms to merchant ships lost in the fog, the seabed is home to the silent remnants of these tragedies. Among them, the wreck of the SS Princess May, which ran aground in 1910 near Juneau, is one of the most photographed in the world.

Divers with a passion for history and adventure are drawn to these wrecks, which offer a unique insight into the maritime history of the region. Rusty hulls, massive anchors, and scattered personal items tell stories of bravery, tragedy, and survival.

If you're a history buff or just curious, this collection of submerged shipwrecks will give you a mesmerizing glimpse into Alaska's maritime past. A natural museum that bears witness to the indomitable strength of nature and human history.

Fact 65 - Beavers, the Architects of Rivers

You've probably heard about the hard work of beavers, but did you know how essential these animals are to Alaska's ecosystem? Let's discover together these incredible architects of rivers.

In Alaska, beavers are more than just rodents. He is a tireless builder, creating dams and ponds that transform river landscapes. These structures, made from branches and mud, not only serve as habitat for the beaver, but they also alter the environment, creating wetlands that promote biodiversity. For example, ponds created by beavers can become habitats for frogs, birds, and a variety of fish.

But their impact doesn't stop there. Beaver dams slow the flow of rivers, allowing the land to better retain water. This helps prevent soil erosion and recharge groundwater.

Next time you're walking by a river in Alaska, take a moment to admire the work of these little architects. Thanks to their ingenuity, beavers play a key role in preserving the balance of Alaska's nature.

Fact 66 - The Grizzly Bear Symphony

Have you ever wondered what Alaska would be like without its iconic grizzly bears? These majestic animals add a touch of wild magic to the natural melody of this region. But there's more to their presence than meets the eye.

Deep in Alaska's vast forests and rugged mountains, grizzly bears play a vital ecological role. By hunting and feeding on salmon during their annual migration, they transport essential nutrients from the ocean to the interior. By leaving behind fish remains, they enrich the soil and promote vegetation growth.

Their role doesn't stop there. By digging into the soil for tubers or insects, they aerate the soil, which benefits the plants. In addition, as apex predators, they regulate the population of other animals, contributing to the balance of the ecosystem.

The next time you hear about Alaskan grizzly bears, remember that they are not only impressive to behold, but also orchestrate a veritable ecological symphony in the Alaskan wilderness.

Fact 67 - Starfish illuminating the seabed

Imagine diving into the cold waters of Alaska and discovering a fairytale world, where the stars are not only in the sky, but also underwater. Starfish, with their varied shapes and colors, are the true jewels of the Alaskan seabed.

These creatures aren't just beautiful to look at. They play a vital role in the marine ecosystem. By feeding on organisms like mussels, they maintain a balance, allowing various species to coexist. Without them, certain populations of organisms could proliferate uncontrollably.

One of the most amazing species you might encounter is the bioluminescent starfish. At night, it emits a soft glow, creating a light show underwater. This bioluminescence is a defense mechanism, deterring predators or attracting prey.

Next time you think of Alaska, remember that its magic isn't limited to its mountains and forests. Underwater, a shimmering universe of starfish awaits you, offering a fascinating view of marine life.

Fact 68 - The Forest That Sings with the Wind

Alaska never ceases to amaze you. Away from the hustle and bustle of the city, if you venture into its dense forests, you'll be able to hear a soft, melodious whisper. It's not an illusion, it's the melody that nature sings to you. Alaskan forests have the peculiarity of "singing" with the wind.

The trees, mainly black and white spruce, have fine, tightly packed needles. When the wind blows through them, they vibrate, creating a soft, soothing melody. It's almost as if each tree has its own voice, and together they form a choir.

This phenomenon is not only beautiful to hear, it is also vital for trees. These vibrations help to dissipate snow accumulated on the branches during the winter, preventing the branches from breaking under the weight.

Next time you're walking through an Alaskan forest, close your eyes and listen. Let yourself be carried away by this natural serenade, a gift that only this wild land can offer you.

Fact 69 - Dolphins Riding the Waves

You've probably seen surfers ride the waves with grace and agility. But did you know that the waters of Alaska offer an equally impressive spectacle? Here, it's the dolphins that lend themselves to the game of surfing, and they do it naturally, without boards!

When large ships pass through the cold waters of Alaska, they generate huge waves in their wake. These waves attract dolphins who rush in with boundless energy. With disconcerting ease, they glide along the crest of the waves, sometimes taking dazzling accelerations thanks to the force of the water.

This behavior is not just a hobby for these sea creatures. "Surfing" allows dolphins to move quickly without expending a lot of energy. It's a clever way to use the power of the sea to their advantage.

So, if you're ever sailing in Alaskan waters, keep an eye out for the waves forming around your ship. You might witness this incredible water dance, where dolphins become the kings of surfing.

Fact 70 - The Frog Orchestra in Summer

If you wander around Alaskan marshes or ponds on balmy summer nights, you'll surely be greeted by an unexpected concert. A natural orchestra made up of frogs offers listeners a unique symphony, mixing rhythmic croaks and aquatic melodies.

These frogs, especially the Alaskan wood frog, use their songs to attract a mate. Each male tries to stand out with a distinct melody, creating a harmonious cacophony that resonates through the night. And it's not just background noise; It's a language of love, with each croak having its own meaning.

While this nightly concert may seem simply entertaining to the human ear, it plays a crucial role in the ecosystem. These songs allow not only reproduction, but also communication between frogs, signaling the presence of predators or other dangers.

The next time you find yourself in Alaska during the summer, take a moment to stop and listen. Let yourself be enveloped by the frog orchestra and feel the magic of nature in harmony.

Fact 71 - The Labyrinth of Braided Rivers

Have you ever heard of braided rivers? Alaska is home to many of them, forming an intricate web that resembles braids seen from the sky. These natural formations are a spectacle in their own right and are characteristic of flat terrain with abundant water flow carrying large volumes of sediment.

The process is fascinating. When the water runs off, it carries with it gravel, sand and sediment. Over time, these materials accumulate, creating temporary islands. The water, looking for the easiest way, then splits into several small streams that meander around these obstacles, giving this braided look.

This phenomenon is particularly noticeable in Denali National Park and Preserve, where the vast expanses allow rivers to flow freely. Braided rivers are not only beautiful to observe, but they also play a vital role in the ecosystem, providing habitats for a variety of species.

Next time you're flying over Alaska or exploring its wilderness, keep an eye out for these hydrographic masterpieces. Their beauty and complexity will remind you of the wonderful ingenuity of nature.

Fact 72 - The Story of the Igloo, the Ice House

Have you heard of the igloo, that rounded structure made of blocks of snow? It is one of the most iconic dwellings in the polar regions, including parts of Alaska. These incredible structures were designed by the Indigenous peoples of the Arctic to brave the biting cold.

Igloos are constructed from carefully hewn blocks of snow, which are stacked in a spiral shape. The choice of snow is crucial: it must be both dense and compact to guarantee insulation. Incredibly, inside an igloo, the temperature can be much milder than outside, despite the fact that it is made entirely of snow.

In Inuit culture, the igloo was often used as a temporary dwelling when travelling for hunting or fishing. Thus, even in the most hostile conditions, these ice houses offered a safe and warm refuge.

So, on your next trip to Alaska, don't hesitate to look for these architectural wonders of snow. You will discover the ingenuity of a people adapted to the most demanding environment.

Fact 73 - The Legend of the Lake Iliamna Monster

Have you ever heard of the mysterious monster of Lake Iliamna? This lake, located in Alaska, is the largest freshwater lake in the state, and according to some, it is home to an enigmatic creature that has been the subject of many local legends.

Accounts vary, but many describe a tall creature with bumps on its back, somewhat evoking the image of Scotland's famous Loch Ness Monster. These stories were often shared by fishermen or locals living near the lake. Some say they have seen huge waves for no apparent reason or gigantic shadows underwater.

Although many researchers and scientists have looked into this legend, no concrete evidence has been found to confirm the existence of this monster. Some believe it could be a species of giant fish or a sturgeon, known for its large size.

Nevertheless, the legend persists, feeding the imagination of locals and visitors alike. If you're going near Lake Iliamna, keep your eyes peeled! Who knows, you might be the next to report a mysterious sighting.

Fact 74 - Ephemeral Ice Sculptures

Alaska, with its frigid temperatures in the winter, offers a unique playground for ice artists. You might be amazed by ephemeral works of art that are born from the imagination of these artists and the purity of the local ice.

Every year, especially during winter festivals, sculptors converge on Alaska to transform simple blocks of ice into stunning creations. These sculptures can range from detailed depictions of animals to abstract shapes, reflecting light in an almost magical way. In 2020, for example, a sculpture depicting a hunting polar bear won a local competition, dazzling viewers with its finesse.

However, the beauty of these works also lies in their ephemeral nature. With the return of spring, these sculptures slowly melt, returning to their liquid state. This transformation is a reminder of the cyclical nature of life and the fragility of art.

Next time you're in Alaska during the winter, don't forget to look for these frozen wonders. They represent not only human creativity, but also the unique interaction between man and nature.

Fact 75 - Starry Nights That Tell Stories

Alaska, away from the bright lights of big cities, has one of the clearest night skies in the world. When you look up at the sky on a clear Alaskan night, you're invited to a sparkling show that has inspired generations of storytellers.

Alaska's indigenous peoples, such as the Yupik and the Inuit, have long searched these starry skies for stories. For them, each constellation has a story to tell. The Big Dipper, for example, is not just a group of stars to them, but represents a series of events, characters, and lessons to be passed on.

More than just a feast for the eyes, these stars also guided travelers through the vast expanses of Alaska. Long before GPS was invented, the stars were the ultimate navigation system.

So, the next time you find yourself under the Alaskan night sky, take a moment to admire. Let yourself be carried away by the stories these stars have to offer, and feel the deep connection that unites man to the universe.

Fact 76 - Giant Crabs of the Deep

Imagine a dark, silent, pressurized world, where creatures the size of toy cars roam the seabed. Alaska is home to those giants of the deep: the red king crabs. These titans can reach an impressive wingspan, sometimes up to nearly three meters from one claw to the next.

Native to the icy waters of the Bering Sea, these crabs are equipped with strong armor and spines that allow them to defend themselves against predators. Their bright red color is not only a beauty to behold, it also plays a crucial role in their camouflage amidst the corals and red algae of the seabed.

If you have the opportunity to taste the delicate flesh of these crabs, you will understand why they are so sought after. They are a culinary specialty and a treasured delicacy for gourmets all over the world.

So, the next time you hear about the wonders of Alaska, don't forget about these impressive deep-sea dwellers, a symbol of the richness and diversity of the region's marine wildlife.

Fact 77 - The Dance of the Fireflies in Summer

Summer in Alaska is a time of wonder, when nature awakens in all its glory. But one of the most beautiful scenes you could ever hope to see is the mesmerizing dance of the fireflies. As soon as the sun goes down, these little creatures light up and transform the night into a symphony of twinkling lights.

Fireflies, or lampyres, aren't just ordinary luminous insects. Their glow is the result of an incredible chemical reaction that occurs inside their bodies. This bioluminescence is a way for them to communicate, attract a mate, and even defend themselves against predators by confusing them.

But why this dance? It's their unique way of seducing. Each species of firefly has its own blinking rhythm, a special light code, to attract the right mate. It's like a masquerade ball, but with lights instead of masks.

So, on your next visit to Alaska in the summer, don't forget to take a moment to admire this luminous parade, a true magic of nature.

Fact 78 - Birds that sing non-stop

Alaska, this vast and wild territory, is home to a multitude of natural curiosities. One of them is the incessant song of certain birds, which, during certain periods, seem never to stop. You're probably wondering why and how this is possible?

The summer period in Alaska is marked by particularly long days, where daylight dominates. These long days stimulate some birds, such as Swainson's nightingale, to sing almost continuously. Their unique vocal mechanism allows them to produce continuous sounds without getting tired.

But why sing so much? The main reason is courtship. These birds sing to attract a mate, mark their territory, and repel other rival males. In this expansive moorland, having a strong and persistent voice can make a difference.

Next time you're visiting Alaska in the summer, keep your ears open. These endless melodies are the echo of a nature in effervescence, seeking to reproduce itself and perpetuate life.

Fact 79 - Deer Wearing Wreaths

Alaska, with its vast wilderness and dense forests, is home to impressive wildlife. Among these inhabitants, there is a peculiar deer that seems to be wearing a real crown. You're intrigued, aren't you? Let me tell you.

The Sitka deer, a subspecies endemic to Alaska, is known for its impressive antlers. These antlers, which grow every year, are like branching fingers, rising proudly above their heads, like royal crowns. But it's not just for showmanship that these deer sport such ornaments.

Antlers play a crucial role in seduction rituals and fights between males. The larger and more branched the antlers, the more likely the deer is to attract a mate or deter rivals. It is nature that offers this magnificent spectacle of dominance and parade.

Next time you're walking through the forests of Alaska, keep your eyes peeled. These majestic deer, wearing their natural crowns, are the living symbol of the wild splendor of this region.

Fact 80 - The Art of Fishing with Eagles

Have you ever seen an eagle in action, diving with deadly precision to catch a wriggling fish? In Alaska, it's a common sight, where bald eagles master the art of fishing with unparalleled grace and skill.

Their keen eyes can spot a fish on the surface of the water even at dizzying altitudes. Once the target is spotted, the eagle adjusts its trajectory, dives at full speed and, with surgical precision, catches the fish with its sharp talons. It's a dance of nature, where every movement counts.

But why Alaska? The crystal clear and abundant waters of fish in this area provide a constant food source for these predators. Places like the Chilkat River are particularly popular, where hundreds of eagles gather each year to take advantage of the salmon bonanza.

Next time you visit Alaska, take some time to observe. The ballet of eagles diving to catch their prey is one of the many natural treasures this place has to offer.

Fact 81 - The Secret Stories of Gemstones

Have you ever wondered where the sparkling gemstones that adorn jewelry and crowns come from? Alaska is full of these treasures, each stone having its own unique story, shaped by time and nature.

One of these stones is jade, the official stone of Alaska. Its hues ranging from pale to dark green are a reflection of the state's vast wilderness landscapes. Imagine a piece of jade, quarried from the rugged mountains, that took thousands of years to form, with each era adding a new layer to its history.

But jade isn't the only hidden treasure. Garnet, with its deep red tones, can be found in winding rivers, sometimes on the surface, waiting for a passerby to discover it. Indeed, the town of Wrangell is famous for its garnet-rich beaches.

The next time you hold one of these stones in your hand, think of its journey from the depths of the Alaskan wilderness to you. Each stone tells a story of bygone eras, pressures and transformations. It's all the magic of Alaska captured in a shimmering sparkle.

Fact 82 - The Incredible Journey of Migrating Caribou

Have you ever heard of the great migrations of animals? Alaska is the scene of one of nature's most spectacular ballets: the caribou migration. These hardy and majestic animals embark on a mammoth journey through harsh terrain and unforgiving climates every year.

The Porcupine caribou herd, for example, travels more than 1,500 km between its wintering and summer areas. Imagine those thousands of caribou, marching in single file, crossing rivers, mountains and tundras, guided by an ancestral instinct. Their determination and endurance are a true testament to the force of nature.

But why such a trip? These migrations are essential for their survival. They seek out new pastures, avoid predators, and find milder weather conditions for calving. Their journey is also punctuated by the seasons and the climatic variations of Alaska.

The next time you look at a map of Alaska, think of these incredible creatures that roam its vast expanses. Their journey is a dance with nature, an ode to life in its purest and wildest form.

Fact 83 - Seal Dance on the Ice

Have you ever seen a graceful creature moving across the ice like a professional dancer? Alaskan seals provide this enchanting spectacle. These mammals, although massive and hardy, move across the ice with astonishing ease and elegance.

When the frozen expanses of Alaska form, many seals, such as the bearded seal, come to rest and feed. Their movements, combining slides and small jumps, seem to be a natural choreography. A striking example is the way they emerge from water holes in the ice, making almost artistic rotations.

But why this "dance"? These movements are actually essential for their survival. By moving quickly and nimbly, they are easier to evade predators and keep their water access holes free of ice, which are essential for breathing and fishing.

The next time you hear about the icy regions of Alaska, imagine these seals, natural dancers, performing on the frozen Arctic stage. Their ballet is a fascinating spectacle of nature not to be missed.

Fact 84 - The Island Where Flowers Talk

Have you ever wondered if nature can tell you stories? In Alaska, there is an island where, it is said, flowers speak. Of course, they don't express themselves in words like we do, but they tell the story of the island in their own unique way.

On this island, the blooming of wildflowers varies according to the seasons and climatic conditions. Each color, each fragrance has its own story. For example, the alpine blueberry, with its delicate blue flowers, is reminiscent of the ancient legends of the Native peoples who inhabited Alaska long before us.

The way these flowers grow, in clusters or singly, in full sun or shade, also gives clues to the peculiarities of the island's soil and climate. And when you take the time to observe and listen, you can almost hear the whisper of centuries past through them.

So, next time you're visiting Alaska, take a moment to head to this mystical island. Let yourself be carried away by the stories these silent flowers are ready to share.

Fact 85 - Reindeer dancing in the snow

Have you ever seen a reindeer dancing? In Alaska, during the winter months, it is common to see reindeer performing amazing dances under the glistening snow. It's not really a dance in the sense we understand it, but their graceful, synchronized movements feel like natural choreography.

These "dances" are actually a way for the reindeer to dig through the snow in search of food. They use their powerful front legs to clear snow and access the lichens below. Their rhythmic movement, coupled with the shimmering snow, gives the impression of a mystical dance.

But it's not just a matter of survival. These times are also opportunities for the reindeer to socialize. The young reindeer learn from their elders by imitating them, thus strengthening the bonds of the group.

The next time you have the chance to visit the snowy lands of Alaska, take a moment to observe this natural dance. It's a sight you'll never forget.

Fact 86 - The Story of Fire Under the Ice

Did you know that Alaska hides a mysterious secret beneath its icy expanses? In the heart of some of its coldest regions, fire smoulders beneath the ice. This astonishing phenomenon is due to the presence of underground hot springs that warm the surface, despite the thick blankets of ice and snow.

These hot springs are the result of geothermal activity in the area. Alaska is located on the Pacific Ring of Fire, an area where plate tectonics create intense volcanic and seismic activity. Thus, the heat of the magma rises to the surface, forming hot springs.

Indigenous peoples discovered these springs millennia ago. To them, these warm waters were both a blessing and a sacred place. They provided a respite from the biting cold, and were often shrouded in legends and myths.

If you're traveling to Alaska, you might be tempted to take a dip in one of these natural pools. But always remember to respect these places, witnesses of an ancient history where fire and ice coexist in harmony.

Fact 87 - Whales Singing Songs

Have you ever heard of singing whales? In Alaska, these giants of the oceans sing intricate, song-like melodies that resonate in the depths. These songs are one of the most fascinating mysteries of marine life.

Each whale song is unique and can last anywhere from a few minutes to more than half an hour. Scientists have discovered that these melodies evolve over time. A whale will never sing exactly the same song from one year to the next. Intriguing, isn't it?

What makes these songs even more incredible is their function. Some believe they are used to attract a mate, while others believe they are a means of communication between whales. For example, in 1977, two humpback whales were recorded near Alaska, and their song, named "Song of the Deep Ocean," fascinated researchers with its complexity.

If you ever get the chance to sail in Alaskan waters, keep an ear out. You could be the privileged witness of one of these underwater concerts, where whales reveal their souls in song.

Fact 88 - Bears Dancing Under the Moon

Have you ever imagined bears dancing in the moonlight? In Alaska, local legends tell of these majestic mammals that, at times, seem to dance on their hind legs. Although it is not a dance in the traditional sense, this vision is both fascinating and mysterious.

These "dances" are actually behaviors that bears use to communicate or express curiosity. Sometimes a bear will stand on its hind legs and make slow circular motions with its front paws, as if it is being carried away by an invisible melody. These gestures can have several meanings, ranging from innocent play to courtship.

Such a vision has inspired many Indigenous peoples. Some say that on full moon nights, the spirits of the ancestors take the form of bears to dance and celebrate life. These legends have shaped generations.

The next time you see a bear in Alaska, imagine it dancing under the moon. It's a poetic way to see the beauty of nature unfold before your eyes.

Fact 89 - The Incredible Journey of Migratory Birds

Have you ever looked up to the sky in Alaska to see a breathtaking sight? Every year, a multitude of migratory birds pass through this state, traveling thousands of miles to find food and shelter. It's a remarkable performance that reveals the incredible endurance of these winged creatures.

A fascinating example is the ruddy godwit, a bird capable of flying nearly 11,000 kilometres without taking a break, connecting directly from New Zealand to Alaska. This is one of the longest known non-stop migrations! During this journey, the godwit depends on its fat reserves and its ability to sleep in flight.

But why do these birds undertake such journeys? For the most part, they migrate to escape the harsh winter conditions and to breed in milder areas. Alaska, with its vast expanses and abundant resources in the summer, is the perfect place for this.

Next time you gaze at the sky in Alaska, think of these winged travelers. They embody the very essence of perseverance and adaptability in the face of nature's challenges.

Fact 90 - The Stars That Tell the Future

Have you ever gazed at the starry sky in Alaska and felt a deep connection to the universe? The stars, bright and enigmatic, have long been the center of stories and beliefs for Alaska Native people. For them, these stars are not mere points of light, but messengers of the future.

The Athabascans, for example, believe that each star is the soul of a deceased person. According to their tradition, by carefully observing the stars, one can receive messages from the ancestors and glimpse omens concerning the future. Their position, brilliance, or movement can reveal everything.

It's not just a matter of superstition or belief. These traditions are rooted in meticulous observations of the stars and celestial phenomena. From the Northern Lights to the constellations, each element has its own meaning, inherited from generation to generation.

Next time you're looking at the night sky in Alaska, think of these ancient legends. Let yourself be carried away by the magic of the stars and maybe, if you pay attention, they will reveal a fragment of your future.

Fact 91 - The Story of Alaska's Early Pioneers

Alaska, this vast wilderness, was not always as populated and accessible as it is today. The first pioneers who set foot on its land were true adventurers, driven by a spirit of discovery. These intrepid individuals were looking for a better life, opportunities, or simply driven by curiosity about the unknown.

Among them were trappers, gold prospectors and explorers from different parts of the world. Take the example of Joe Juneau and Richard Harris, two gold miners who, in 1880, discovered gold near what is now Juneau, the state capital. Their discovery sparked a veritable gold rush, drawing thousands of people to Alaska.

But the arrival of these pioneers was not without its challenges. The harsh weather conditions, the inhospitable territory and the wildlife encounters tested their endurance and determination. Despite this, they persevered, establishing the first communities and laying the foundation for modern Alaska.

Next time you're walking in Alaska, think of these pioneers. Their courage and determination have shaped this magnificent state, making it accessible to all who dream of adventure.

Fact 92 - The Mystery of Moving Stones

Have you ever heard of stones that move on their own? Alaska holds many mysteries, and one of the most intriguing is that of moving stones. These rocks, sometimes large, move inexplicably, leaving behind traces on the ground, as if they were animated by a will of their own.

Some of these stones are found in remote areas of Alaska, off the beaten path. Researchers have long been puzzled by this phenomenon. Several theories have been put forward, ranging from the intervention of animals to natural phenomena, such as freezing and thawing of the ground, which could cause the stones to move.

More recent studies suggest that a combination of specific weather conditions and the formation of thin ice patches may be behind this movement. When the wind blows over these ice patches, it can cause the stones to move.

Nevertheless, even with these explanations, the mystery remains unsolved for many. So, if you ever find yourself in Alaska, keep an eye out. Maybe you'll be lucky enough to see these stones in motion and add your own chapter to this riddle.

Fact 93 - The Island Where Time Stood Still

Do you know that island in Alaska where it seems like time has never advanced? This mysterious land is called the Isle of Oblivion. It is so isolated that most of its landscapes and ecosystems have changed little in thousands of years.

When you set foot on this island, it's like stepping back in time. Giant trees, centuries old, dominate the landscape, offering a panorama of wild beauty. The fauna is as abundant as it was in prehistoric times. You might even feel like you're hearing the distant echoes of the Indigenous peoples who lived there long before the first explorers arrived.

What makes this island even more fascinating is the almost complete absence of human intervention. No roads have been built, no modern buildings have been erected. It is a sanctuary of nature, preserved by its own isolation and deliberate efforts to protect it.

If you ever have the opportunity to visit the Isle of Oblivion, you will feel a deep respect for this window into the distant past. It will remind you how precious and ephemeral our world is.

Fact 94 - The Story of the City Lost Under the Ice

Have you ever heard of that legend that whispers that an ancient city is buried under the massive glaciers of Alaska? The City of Icetown, as it is known, would have been a prosperous metropolis thousands of years ago.

According to accounts, the people of Icetown were skilled craftsmen who had established extensive trade routes. However, a particularly harsh winter would have enveloped the city, quickly covering it with snow and ice. And over the centuries, glaciers continued to expand, completely engulfing the city.

Modern explorers, attracted by this legend, have launched several expeditions to find the traces of Icetown. Although no concrete evidence has been found to date, some have reported discovering ancient artifacts near glacial areas, fueling speculation about the actual existence of this city.

If this story fascinates you, you're not alone. Many continue to hope that one day, Icetown's secrets will be revealed, offering a glimpse into life in Alaska millennia ago.

Fact 95 - Eagles Fishing with Their Claws

Did you know that Alaska is home to some of the world's largest eagles? These majestic birds don't just soar through the sky, they are also outstanding fishermen.

The bald eagle, in particular, is known for its impressive fishing skills. With surgical precision, it dives into the water, extends its powerful talons, and catches fish with disconcerting ease. These sharp, strong claws allow it to firmly grasp its prey, even if it is slippery and restless.

But it's not just a question of strength. The eagle also has exceptional vision that allows it to spot fish from great heights. This ability, coupled with its speed and agility, makes it a formidable predator.

Next time you're in Alaska, keep your eyes up. You might have the chance to observe this incredible natural spectacle of an eagle in the middle of the act of fishing. And believe me, it's a moment you'll never forget.

Fact 96 - Dolphins Drawing in the Water

Have you ever observed strange shapes and patterns in the water and wondered where they came from? In the icy waters of Alaska, some dolphins have a unique way of "drawing" in the ocean.

These dolphins use bubbles to create circles, spirals, and other intriguing patterns. It's not just a game or a demonstration of their ability to manipulate their environment. These aquatic drawings have a specific purpose: they are used to trap fish by circling them, thus facilitating their capture.

But this behavior is not purely utilitarian. It seems that these bubble designs are also a form of communication between dolphins. By studying these patterns, one can guess if a school of fish is nearby or if a potential hazard lurks in the vicinity.

So, on your next visit to Alaska, take a close look at the surface of the water. You could witness these ephemeral masterpieces drawn by dolphins, combining both art and survival in a mesmerizing aquatic ballet.

Fact 97 - Flowers that open at midnight

You've probably heard of the midnight sun in Alaska, but did you know that there are flowers that choose this magical moment to bloom? It's a phenomenon that can only be found in certain polar regions of the globe, and Alaska is one of them.

In these areas, during certain times of the year, the sun never really sets. As a result, some plants have adapted to this peculiarity and changed their flowering cycle. Instead of blooming during the day, these flowers wait for the soft light of the midnight sun to show off their splendor.

One of these flowers is the "Midnight Lily". Its beautiful white corolla opens only when the sun is lowest in the sky, providing a dazzling natural spectacle in contrast to the deep blue of Alaskan summer nights.

If you have the opportunity to visit Alaska during these special months, don't miss this show. Sit down, breathe deeply, and observe these flowers that, like night lights, light up the night with their beauty.

Fact 98 - The Dance of the Sea Lions Under the Waves

Maybe you've already witnessed the grace of sea lions gliding across the surface of the water, but do you know their secret ballet beneath the waves? The icy waters of Alaska are home to a fascinating world where these creatures move with incredible ease.

Alaskan sea lions, despite their rugged appearance and imposing size, are extraordinary swimmers. They can perform spins, spirals and slides, often playing with underwater currents. These moves aren't just for fun; They are also used to surprise their prey or escape predators.

The most mesmerizing sight is during courtships. Males perform elaborate dances to seduce females, displaying their agility and strength. This water ballet is a perfect blend of power and grace.

If you're diving in Alaskan waters, take a moment to observe these sea dancers. Their underwater dance will remind you of the wild and pure beauty of nature that prevails in Alaska.

Fact 99 - The Story of Talking Forests

Have you ever walked through a forest and felt that it spoke to you? In Alaska, this feeling is amplified by the ancient history of the woods and the tales associated with them. Alaska's forests aren't just made up of trees; they are imbued with the voices of the past.

Alaska Native peoples have long believed that forests are inhabited by spirits. These beliefs have given rise to many legends, such as that of the Kushtaka, a shape-shifting spirit that can take on the appearance of a man or an otter. The ancients say that if you listen carefully, you can hear the whispers of these spirits in the rustling of leaves.

Forests are also full of signs left behind by animals, birds and insects. These markings, whether it's scraped bark or an abandoned feather, tell stories of survival, hunting, and everyday life.

The next time you're in a forest in Alaska, close your eyes, listen, and feel the living history around you. Every tree, every stone has a story to tell you.

Fact 100 - The Mystery of the Lakes That Glow in the Night

Imagine walking by a lake in Alaska, and suddenly, at the height of the night, you see the lake light up like a starry sky. This phenomenon, as strange as it may seem, is very real and part of the natural wonders of Alaska.

The reason for this mysterious flicker comes from microorganisms called bioluminescent dinoflagellates. These tiny creatures emit light when the water is agitated, creating a surprising light show. This phenomenon, although more common in seas and oceans, can also be observed in some freshwater lakes in Alaska, especially on hot summer nights.

This bioluminescence has fascinated local people for generations. Indigenous legends speak of dancing spirits who use the lake as their mirror, reflecting their celestial brilliance.

The next time you find yourself wandering by a lake in Alaska at night, take a moment to observe. You could witness one of the most beautiful natural puzzles of this wild state.

Conclusion

And there you have it, dear reader, our incredible journey through the wild and mysterious lands of Alaska is coming to an end. As you walk through these pages, you've discovered natural wonders, captivating tales, and mysteries that make this state so unique and enchanting. Hopefully, each fact has amazed you as much as it has amazed us when we discovered it.

As you close this book, keep in mind that Alaska, with its raw beauty and untamed nature, is a powerful reminder of the splendor of our planet. It is a place where the land, the water, the sky, and all the creatures that reside there tell stories of adventure, survival, and coexistence.

Maybe you'll be inspired to visit Alaska one day, to see these wonders with your own eyes and create your own memories. Or maybe these stories have simply broadened your horizons, reminding you that the world is vast, diverse, and always surprising.

Thank you for joining us on this journey. Wherever you go next, may you always keep curiosity and wonder at the heart of your adventures. Goodbye, and may your discoveries still be as incredible as those of Alaska!

Marc Dresgui

Quiz

1) What is special about eagles in Alaska while hunting?

    a) They use tools to fish.
    b) They fish with their claws.
    c) They dive at supersonic speeds.
    d) They hunt in groups.

2) What natural phenomenon can cause hallucinations in reindeer?

    a) Acid rain.
    b) Volcanic eruptions.
    c) Mushrooms.
    d) Flower pollen.

3) Why do some lakes in Alaska glow in the night?

    a) Because of bioluminescent algae.
    b) They are filled with fireflies.
    c) Because of the reflection of the moon.
    d) They are contaminated with chemicals.

4) What animal is known to draw patterns in the water in Alaska?

    a) Sea lions.
    b) Seals.

c) Dolphins.

d) Clownfish.

5) What is special about the flowers of the island in Alaska?

a) They change color.

b) They only open at midnight.

c) They can walk.

d) They make sounds.

6) Why are whales in Alaska special?

a) They never migrate.

b) They are the largest in the world.

c) They sing songs.

d) They don't have teeth.

7) What is special about the forests in Alaska according to local legends?

a) They are haunted.

b) They can talk.

c) They move.

d) They are eternally covered in snow.

8) How are bears often seen on clear nights?

a) On the hunt.

b) In hibernation.

c) Dancing under the moon.

d) Swimming.

9) What is special about stones in Alaska?

a) They float.

b) They are magnetic.

c) They move.

d) They glow in the dark.

10) What is the city that is said to have been lost in Alaska made of?

a) Golden.

b) Diamonds.

c) Ice.

d) Precious stones.

11) What is the weather like on a particular Alaskan island?

a) It is reversed.

b) He stopped.

c) It's accelerated.

d) It is unpredictable.

12) What is the peculiar dance of sea lions in Alaska?

a) On dry land.
b) Beneath the waves.
c) On the ice.
d) In the trees.

13) How does fire appear under the ice in Alaska?

a) Because of volcanic eruptions.
b) Because of the sun's rays.
c) Because of the campfires.
d) Because of the lightning.

14) How is the future in Alaska perceived by looking at the sky?

a) Through the clouds.
b) Through the stars.
c) Through the Northern Lights.
d) Through meteors.

15) What are the first inhabitants of Alaska called?

a) The Vikings.
b) The Pioneers.
c) The Eskimos.
d) The Nomads.

16) What are Alaskan flowers compared to because of their communication?

    a) To the stars.

    b) To animals.

    c) To human beings.

    d) To insects.

17) What is the longest day in Alaska during the summer?

    a) 12 hours.

    b) 6 p.m.

    c) 24 hours.

    d) 8 p.m.

18) What are the waves created by sea lions in Alaska?

    a) Calm.

    b) Giant.

    c) Rhythmic.

    d) Fast.

19) What celestial phenomenon is most visible in Alaska?

    a) Shooting stars.

    b) The solar eclipse.

c) The Aurora Borealis.

d) The planets.

20) Why do some animals migrate to Alaska?

a) To escape predators.

b) To find food.

c) To hibernate.

d) To reproduce.

Answers

1) **What is special about eagles in Alaska while hunting?**

   Correct answer: b) They fish with their claws.

2) **What natural phenomenon can cause hallucinations in reindeer?**

   Correct answer: c) Mushrooms.

3) **Why do some lakes in Alaska glow in the night?**

   Correct answer: a) Because of bioluminescent algae.

4) **What animal is known to draw patterns in the water in Alaska?**

   Correct answer: (c) Dolphins.

5) **What is special about the flowers of the island in Alaska?**

   Correct answer: (b) They open only at midnight.

6) Why are whales in Alaska special?

Correct answer: c) They sing songs.

7) What is special about the forests in Alaska according to local legends?

Correct answer: b) They can speak.

8) How are bears often seen on clear nights?

Correct answer: c) Dancing under the moon.

9) What is special about stones in Alaska?

Correct answer: c) They are moving.

10) What is the city that is said to have been lost in Alaska made of?

Correct answer: c) Ice.

11) What is the weather like on a particular Alaskan island?

Correct answer: b) He stopped.

12) **What is the peculiar dance of sea lions in Alaska?**

Correct answer: b) Under the waves.

13) **How does fire appear under the ice in Alaska?**

Correct answer: a) Because of volcanic eruptions.

14) **How is the future in Alaska perceived by looking at the sky?**

Correct answer: b) Through the stars.

15) **What are the first inhabitants of Alaska called?**

Correct answer: (b) The Pioneers.

16) **What are Alaskan flowers compared to because of their communication?**

Correct answer: (c) To human beings.

17) **What is the longest day in Alaska during the summer?**

Correct answer: c)24 hours.

18) What are the waves created by sea lions in Alaska?

Correct answer: c)Rhythmic.

19) What celestial phenomenon is most visible in Alaska?

Correct answer: c) The Aurora Borealis.

20) Why do some animals migrate to Alaska?

Correct answer: b) To find food.

Made in United States
Orlando, FL
21 November 2023